HOW TO DEAL WITH ALCOHOLICS AND ALCOHOLISM

Steps And Tips Dealing With An Alcoholic

By: Sky Stevens

Table Of Contents

Introduction

Are you trying to deal with an alcoholic, a friend or relative that alcoholism is their way of living? It can be really difficult living or dealing with a close friend or a family member that is drinking with the intent to become drunk one or two times a week (and in a lot of cases, daily). If you find yourself in this situation, I believe my book will help you out. I will first share two of my experiences and stories, and then I will offer suggestions as to what I feel may help you. I, the author of this book, have lived and dealt with several alcoholics in my life. I know the symptoms, and I know how to deal with them. Here are two true stories of mine:

Several years back, I had an aunt who needed a place to stay because she was coming from a halfway house. She was previously in Tent City Maricopa County for driving drunk more than once. When she left the halfway house, she asked to stay in my extra room. I allowed it for a temporary situation in hopes she would clean herself up.

Night after night I would come home in the evening to see her passed out on my living room floor. She was surrounded by open beer cans or bottles from a twelve pack that she had drunk in its entirety. I had no idea where she was getting her money for her beer habit. I was only in my early twenties at the time, living independently, and having to deal with an aunt who was in her forties that acted like a child. It was unbelievable! I would try to talk with her and consistently pleaded with her, and it resulted in my threatening to kick her out if she did not clean up. Unfortunately, my aunt never cleaned up. I spoke with my grandmother who lived in another state about her daughters drinking habits. After speaking with her, I soon found out my grandmother was sending my aunt money under the impression it was for her living expenses. Wrong! My aunt was taking advantage of me and my hospitality of living rent-free and even ran up my bills that she still has not paid back today. At one time, she even took my Texaco gas card and put four hundred dollars on it for her gas and beer purchases. Having no knowledge she had done this, I had to quickly pay that credit card off so it would not hurt my credit score.

I told my grandmother that if she wanted to support her daughter's habits then her daughter would need to move in with her. After several months of trying to get her to move out, she finally did. I felt tremendous weight lifted from my shoulders. I was happy once again.

Here is my second story:

My brother, as of today, is an alcoholic. He will drink to get drunk at least twice a week. Being that we are only one year apart, in age, we grew up together and were very close. When we were in our high school years he never would get wasted or drunk. He was an honor roll student with high GPA.

Unfortunately, something changed in him when we were in our early twenties. The backsliding began and drinking became a way of life. It even cost him dearly when he received two D.U.I.'s. Today, in our late thirties, he is still drinking and gets drunk on a weekly basis. When he gets drunk he can have a violent temper. His mind overreacts to harmless situations.

Here is just one example: I am a married man. One night, I was at my mother's home visiting for a few hours. My brother was there with an ex-girlfriend of his that just came into town. My brother was well into a few beers at this time. His ex-girlfriend, let's call her Susan, approached me while I was at my mother's computer minding my own business. Susan asked me if my wife and I would like to go out with her and my brother. My brother witnessed her from a distance speaking with me, but did not hear our conversation. My brother immediately approached us asking, "What the hell you two talking about?" Susan told him what she had asked me. My brother glared at me and waited till she left before confronting me. As I sat at my mother's computer, he came up to me, hovered over me with a psychotic look in his eyes and threatened me. He would not let up about it. My mother and Susan both were trying to now calm him down but he would not back down. He wanted to fight.

Let's just say the cops were called and the cops had to take care of my brother's drunkenness. I left for home and have not spoken with my brother for several months now. The deal is we speak when he goes to rehab or quits the bottle, on his own.

Yes, it does hurt, because my brother and I grew up together. We were always there for each other and never would have seen the day where our brotherly bond would be compromised by the riveting effects of alcohol. All of that has changed now.

Here are some tips…

You Cant Change this Person

If you are dealing with someone suffering from an addiction to alcohol, please understand that you alone can not change his or her behavior. The only person who holds that power is the alcoholic themselves. They have to come to the conclusion that they have a problem on their own. This is not like asking your friend to get up and go to the gym. Alcoholism is an addiction, and a really powerful one at that. To you it may seem like an easy habit to drop, but to them it's extremely difficult. They have become dependent on this substance, so asking him or her to stop drinking is like asking them to stop eating. Eliminating this behavior requires a major lifestyle change. Don't expect the impossible.

1. Do NOT Enable the Alcoholic

The worst thing you can do for an alcoholic is enable their habits and behaviors. This is not an easy thing to do, especially if you are close with the person. Hold your ground and let them hit their rock bottom. To fully understand the consequences of their lifestyle, they have to face them head on and they have to do it alone. I can't tell you how many times I bailed my son out of jail for a D.U.I. At the time I felt I was helping him, but I was just allowing him to continue the behavior. In his eyes, he was free to go back to drinking because I would always be there to bail him out. It was only when I forced him to deal with his actions that he finally began to realize he had a problem.

Please don't make the same mistake I did. Do not come to the person's rescue. You are not a superhero, this is not your job. Do not bail them out of jail, give them money to fund their habit, or even offer them a place to stay. In fact, do your best to stay out of the person's life altogether until they get help. The stress and heartache does nobody any good. Once they agree to attend A.A. meetings and work on overcoming their addiction, those doors may be opened. Should they give up on their recovery at any point, you'll have to shut those doors once again.

2. Lying is Part of the Alcoholics Game

Just like any other person suffering from an addiction, alcoholics will frequently tell lies. Why? Because the alcoholic knows that they have to lie in order to continue the behavior. They're well aware that you disapprove of their lifestyle and would rather avoid you giving them a hard time. Try not to confront the alcoholic about their lies as they're never going to fess up. If the person is drunk, do not expect any kind of truthful responses. You'll only get frustrated or aggravated. Always keep in mind that until the person decides they have a problem, they will be living in a constant state of denial.

3. Avoid Arguments with an Alcoholic

Arguing with a person who has been drinking is never a good idea, regardless of whether or not they have a problem with alcohol. At this point, the alcoholic is at a heightened emotional state and can be easily set off. This is definitely not the time to talk about anything serious. If you feel an argument coming on, do everything you can to either avoid or get yourself out of this situation as quickly as possible. Using a calm, soothing tone of voice can help ease a situation. If it exacerbates and you find yourself backed into a corner, just begin agreeing with everything they say. Things could get out of hand if you continue to disagree with them. If you really need to speak with the alcoholic about something serious, please wait until they are sober. Remember, though, that they will still be in a state of denial.

Alcoholism vs. Drug Addiction

People have long debated whether or not you can really call alcohol an addictive drug. After all, there are millions of people around the world who consume it everyday, but are not addicted. Generally, any kind of hard drug, like cocaine, is not used recreationally like alcohol is. This may be why people have such a hard time seeing it in this light. But when you look at the facts, alcoholism fits the bill as an addictive and equally harmful drug.

1. An alcoholic is physically dependent on the substance.

2. Many people lose their lives because of the abuse of alcohol.

3. In order to get the desired results, an alcoholic must continually increase their consumption.

Much like a person who has overcome an addiction to a hard drug, a recovering alcoholic can get hooked again with just one slip. They have become physically and mentally dependent upon the alcohol and this is a permanent dependence. There is no cure. Should a recovering alcoholic fall off the bandwagon, they will have start again from square one.

There are treatment centers that focus on alcoholism and will help establish a new lifestyle for the alcoholic. The facility will be free of the substance and psychological advice is offered. However, it's the group therapy sessions that tend to help alcoholics stay on the right track.

When most people think of group therapy, Alcoholics Anonymous (also known as A.A.) tends to come to mind. Meetings are organized in cities all over the country to help recovering alcoholics stay sober. So many recovering alcoholics will tell you it's these meetings that keep them on track.

It may be hard to believe, but if alcohol was just discovered today, it would never make it to store shelves. The substance itself is toxic in nature! However, because there is such a deep, rich history embedded in the alcohol industry, it would be near impossible to place a ban on it as so many jobs would be lost. And while Western governments are busy fighting the war on drugs all around the world, people are dying from alcohol abuse on a daily basis. In fact, more people lose their lives to alcohol daily than they they do to drug-related addictions or crimes.

What makes it worse is that alcoholism not only affects the person addicted, but everyone else around them. This includes their friends, their family and even utter strangers. Because alcoholics are in such denial of their problem, they tend to believe they are "a-ok" to drive. Unfortunately, this results in thousands of deaths each year because of intoxicated drivers. I'd be willing to bet that you know someone who has either had an accident, or been pulled over because of drunk driving. It's a sad reality and only the families of the victims are the ones left to suffer. So, you see, the only difference between alcohol and any other drug is that alcohol is legal. You can find it on many local grocery store shelves. Yet it's just as addictive, deadly and costly as any illegal drug.

Is Alcoholism Really a Disease?

In short, yes, alcoholism is a disease. Many people have a hard time grasping this concept because alcoholism does not really act like a disease in the traditional sense. Yet, the medical industry recognizes alcoholism as a chronic and progressive one. We define a disease as a malfunctioning organ or body system that, in turn, can cause infections, deficiencies, illness or death. From a technical standpoint, you can see why some people refuse to accept alcoholism as such.

However, the disease lies in the mental and physical dependence on alcohol. And just like any other disease, there are factors that cause its onset, symptoms associated with the condition and treatment options. Seeing as alcohol is often served at special occasions, holidays and parties, there is a major social factor in the development of alcoholism. Science has also found genetic factors that make certain people more prone to developing alcoholism.

Someone who lacks the ability to control their consumption of alcohol, has a great tolerance of alcohol's effects, or often craves the substance may be exhibiting symptoms of alcoholism. When an alcoholic is unable to get their fix, they will begin to experience withdrawal symptoms. This includes mood swings, vomiting, insomnia, irritability and hand tremors. It's possible to include denial of having a problem as yet another symptom of alcoholism. Because the alcoholic is in such denial of their condition, an intervention is often needed to try and sway them to pursue treatment. There are some cases where an alcoholic will come to this conclusion on their own, but unless they are allowed to hit rock bottom this is unlikely to happen. And even then, it can be rare.

When the alcoholic does decide to enter treatment, they will typically go through a detoxification process, begin speaking with a counselor about their addiction, and attend group therapy sessions for support and any other treatments needed for medical problems. Remember that those suffering from alcoholism have a permanent physical and mental addiction that gets progressively worse over time.

If the alcoholic fails to seek treatment, their situation can become fatal. Before it gets to this stage, often times their alcohol consumption will begin to disrupt their ability to carry
out a normal existence. They will find themselves unable to hold a job, destroying friendships, and suffering from alcohol related health issues. Unfortunately, the negative consequences will often fail to affect an alcoholic and they will continue to binge drink.

Please keep in mind that alcoholism and "drinking problems" is not the same thing. Alcoholism is the most deadly form of alcohol abuse and the victim is unable to control their consumption of the substance. There are individuals who binge drink and cause themselves all kinds of problems, both medically and legally, but are still able to control their consumption of alcohol. They may not have developed alcoholism yet, but they may if they continue down that road.

Alcoholism Treatment – When Rehab is Necessary

Alcoholics Anonymous, or A.A., has helped bring awareness to the treatment options for alcoholism. These rehabilitation programs are vital to keeping recovering alcoholics on the right path. They can also return hope to an alcoholic whose life is on the verge of falling to pieces.

For some alcoholics, rehab is the only option they have. They've reached the point where they've destroyed everything that's important to them. Their job has been lost, their family has been ripped apart and their friends have abandoned them. Others are living in an atmosphere that only continues to enable them to drink. These individuals have no other choice but to enter a rehabilitation facility.

Rehab is where they'll finally be presented with a real solution to their addiction. One they could never receive on their own. It's here that they'll be able to truly learn the reasons why they drink. Many have never really had a healthy relationship with alcohol in the first place.

Remember, checking into rehab for alcohol shouldn't be an act of desperation. In fact, seeking treatment before the problem exasperates may prevent any irreversible consequences like a separated family, lost employment, or a destroyed marriage.

If you suspect that someone you know may be suffering from alcoholism, don't be reluctant to check out some of the facilities in your area. So many alcoholics' lives have been saved with simple, yet effective alcohol rehabilitation programs. While in treatment, the alcoholic will learn how to live in an alcohol-free environment and also become educated about their disease.

Treating Alcoholism and its Causes

Alcoholism does not discriminate. It can affect anyone of any age, gender or race. So many teens become addicted to alcohol, regardless that the legal age to drink is twenty-one. Peer pressure often places these teens in a position where they find it hard to say no to a drink, or even drugs. They have that desire to fit in no matter the consequences. These social pressures have a big part in substance abuse problems with the teen population.

Many young adults between the ages of twelve and twenty have a problem with abusing alcohol. Because these teens are so young, they stand a greater risk of gaining a severe dependency on the substance and may eventually need some sort of intervention to get them into treatment. These damaging behaviors become all that much harder to abandon as time goes on and the fallout will surely affect the teen's ability to lead a normal life.

An adolescent who has become addicted to alcohol will find it extremely difficult to function properly at school and, in turn, their academics will suffer. It's imperative that the teen seeks out alcohol treatment immediately. Because teens tend to have different reasons for drinking, their treatment will also be different than an adult's.

But what causes a teen to begin drinking in the first place? Peer pressure is often the culprit. When an adult becomes dependent on alcohol, they are generally trying to escape reality. It relieves their stress, calms their nerves and makes them forget all about their problems. For teenagers, they are looking to fit in with their peers. If their friends or popular kids are drinking, they will want to do the same. Because the causes for alcoholism amongst teens are so different from adults, their treatments must also be different.

When a teenager enters alcohol treatment, it's important for the program to be appropriate for their age and should, ideally, include their family in the process. If there is a family history of alcohol abuse, the entire family may need to work together to successfully eliminate the destructive behavior. This may be a huge factor in the reason why the teen turned to alcohol to begin with. In the most severe cases of alcohol abuse, a teen will need to stay at the rehabilitation facility.

While the treatment itself may differ for teens and adults, there is one thing that rings true for both: success is completely dependent upon the individual's will and commitment to their recovery. Professionals will be by their side anytime, day or night to get them through this troubling time. However, it is still up to the alcoholic to remain dedicated to the treatment process.

There are many groups, like Alateen, Al-Anon and, of course, Alcoholics Anonymous that can help a teen recover from alcohol abuse. These self-help groups will supply them with positive role models. Others attending the meetings have been in their shoes and they can relate to their feelings. This supportive community will be a wonderful outlet for the teen to open up about their issues. If the teen begins attending meetings before the alcohol abuse gets to the intervention stage, it might help them realize that they are headed on a deadly path.

Alcohol Treatment Centers Will Get You Back on Track

Experts have long stated that both alcoholism and drug addiction is more prevalent in big cities than small towns. Some research supports this statement, but there are still reports with varying conclusions. Regardless of their location, alcoholism still affects many individuals. In fact, 1 out of 3 citizens has some kind of alcohol related addiction! The level of abuse ranges from occasional to constant.

Because this is such a growing problem, a lot of work has been put into raising awareness about the need of treatment centers for alcoholism. Nowadays, there are many programs available is most cities or towns. In fact, they have specialized centers for adolescents and even CEOs.

Recognition of the problem is the first step, treatment and recovery are the second

More often than not, it is a family member, friend, or employer that recognizes a person has an addiction to alcohol. In any case, it's the acknowledgment that there is a problem that's the first step to seeking treatment. A sudden decline in an employee's performance, frequent absences, or late arrivals will certainly catch the attention of an employer. Sometimes all it takes is a few late, intoxicated homecomings to cause a family member or friend to become concerned.

Perhaps the biggest sign that a person is in need of treatment, is their utter lack of recognition that there's a problem. An alcoholic lives in denial. They absolutely do not believe they are addicted to the substance. Meanwhile, they are spending a lot of their time and money on drinking at bars or other alcohol serving establishments.

If a you, a loved one, or friend has a problem with alcohol, please pursue treatment as soon as possible. In doing so, you'll prevent the disease from taking over your life. If you have a job, you can check with your employer for options, or you may get in touch with a
local health organization to see if there are any free treatment programs available. The sooner you can seek out help, the sooner you can get on the road to recovering.

Again, alcoholism does not discriminate. It doesn't matter your age, gender or class. The good news is, over time alcohol treatment programs have evolved and offer different ways to reach recovery. There are even exclusive camps, therapists and support groups that can help you find success. Alcohol rehab has never been so accommodating.

There are individuals who shy away from getting treatment because they are afraid of how others will perceive them. In the past, society viewed both the traditional treatment programs and their participants in a negative way. These new treatment programs, however, have changed people's point of view. In fact, it is now seen as a sign of strength to enter such a program.

Perhaps one of the most groundbreaking programs are the new rehabilitation ranches that been established over the last few years. They give those who are looking to get help a chance to spend a lot of up close and personal time with licensed professionals in a relaxed and positive environment. The program is still focus on what's causing the addiction and attempts to find a solution. What makes these ranches so unique is that on top of the traditional treatment routes, they also incorporate relaxing activities and group exercises into the program. Hiking and horseback riding are just some of the things participants are able to do. They also have group activities that can include building homes for low income families. These kinds of exercises help to relieve the stresses of overcoming addiction.

In some way, shape, or form alcoholism affects everyone. Whether it's you suffering, a family member, friend, colleague or spouse, there are alcohol treatment programs available that can help you begin the recovery process.

The Effects of Alcoholic Drinks and Related Health Issues

For centuries, societies have used alcohol as a way to celebrate occasions. Be it a victory in war, a wedding, birthday or holiday, we have long been using alcohol to bring "life" to a party. Modern society still holds these same views and believes that certain occasions warrant the serving of alcoholic drinks. It helps guests relax and "cut-loose."

Alcohol is the result of the fermentation of vegetables, grains or fruits. This process uses yeast or other bacteria to convert the sugar in these foods into alcohol. This is the same substance that is used to create detergents and cleansers. Alcohol itself acts as a depressant that slows the nervous system and works as a sedative. This is why people drink alcohol to relax, or unwind. It calms nerves and relieves anxiety when taken in small quantities.

However, when consumed in large quantities, it can cause confusion, slurred speech, blurry vision, poor judgment, uncoordinated movements and even loss of consciousness. When extreme amounts of the substance are consumed, it can cause alcohol poisoning which may induce a coma or lead to death. Because alcohol is absorbed straight into the bloodstream, it can cause damage to organs or cause cancer.

And while many people are aware of these repercussions, they continue to drink alcohol. But why? The media may be partly to blame. Children are exposed to alcohol advertisements and young adults watch films that glorify the use of the substance. It's seen as a way to relax, fit in with peers and "the thing to do" while you're young. These films and advertisements show people enjoying a few drinks with friends or family and, in turn, depict alcohol in a positive light. In actuality, there is nothing positive about this pastime. When people drink too much, they tend to do things they regret because their judgment is so poor. And because it damages the nervous system, it can cause people to vomit or do a number of other embarrassing things. Not to mention they'll be suffering through a hangover after the alcohol has worn off.

What's so alarming is that research has shown that many deaths among teenagers is alcohol related. Whenever an individual consumes alcohol, be it a teenager or adult, there
is a great risk of the individual being involved in an automobile accident, homicide or suicide.

Did you know that every thirty minutes a person dies from an alcohol related car accident? Those who are intoxicated have impaired judgment and motor skills, so they are at an extreme risk of causing an accident. Unfortunately, many of those accidents result in death. A driver under the influence poses a risk to not only themselves, but other drivers and pedestrians.

An alcoholic is also at a greater risk of attempting or committing suicide. Statistics show that more than one-third of suicide incidents were committed by an individual who was alcohol dependent. This risk is amplified with age. Research conducted by Alcoholism: Clinical and Experimental Research has shown that the risk of committing suicide was greater among middle-aged and elderly alcoholics versus young adults who were dependent.

When a person consumes dangerous amounts of alcohol, they also stand the risk of developing so many other health issues including cancer or diabetes. Furthermore, the body is unable to absorb appropriate amounts of nutrients and because alcoholics don't usually follow a healthy diet, they cause further harm to their bodies. Health issues caused by alcohol should not be taken lightly and serve as a reminder that you should keep your drinking to a minimum.

Treatment for Alcoholism – What is the twelve-step program?

For decades, twelve-step programs have been the foundation for the process of recovering from not just alcoholism, but many other addictions as well. This program was created back in 1935 by Bill Wilson and Dr. Bob Smith, who happened to be alcoholics themselves. A.A.'s roots are set in spiritual principles as well as the idea that the alcoholic will need support from their peers throughout their lifetime to stay on the right track. Recovering is a life-long process and requires the assistance of others who have been down the same path and have similar experiences. This twelve-step program has also been adopted by other groups like NA (Narcotics Anonymous) and CA (Cocaine Anonymous).

In 1939, Alcoholics Anonymous: The Story of How More Than One Hundred Men Have Recovered from Alcoholism was published. The book contains these twelve-steps which act as a guide of how an alcoholic can overcome their addiction and remain in the recovery stage. Below are the twelve-steps as published by www.aa.org.

1. We admitted we were powerless over alcohol—that our lives had become unmanageable.
2. Came to believe that a Power greater than ourselves could restore us to sanity.
3. Made a decision to turn our will and our lives over to the care of God as we understood Him.

4. Made a searching and fearless moral inventory of ourselves.

5. Admitted to God, to ourselves, and to another human being the exact nature of our wrongs.

6. We're entirely ready to have God remove all these defects of character.

7. Humbly asked Him to remove our shortcomings.

8. Made a list of all persons we had harmed, and became willing to make amends to them all.

9. Made direct amends to such people wherever possible, except when to do so would injure them or others.

10) Continued to take personal inventory and when we were wrong promptly admitted it.

11) Sought through prayer and meditation to improve our conscious contact with God as we understood Him, praying only for knowledge of His will for us and the power to carry that out.

12) Having had a spiritual awakening as the result of these steps, we tried to carry this message to alcoholics, and to practice these principles in all our affairs.

Twelve-step programs really try to encourage acknowledgment of the addiction. Admitting that you have a problem is key. Saying the words out loud really puts things into perspective and begins to make changes psychologically. This is why members of A.A. meetings state their name and what addiction they suffer from, i.e. "Hello, my name is Stacy and I'm an alcoholic." This expression is widely recognized and now incorporated into other twelve-step programs. In order to stay sober, it's advised that group members continue to attend meetings and share experiences with others who have the same addiction.

So, what exactly do these twelve-steps mean? The list above may seem a little too complicated, or technical, so let's break it down.

1: Acknowledgment
The alcoholic has admitted that they have a problem that they can no longer handle on their own.

Step 2: Belief in a higher power
The belief that someone higher than yourself (God) can help you return to a normal life.

Step 3: Submitting to a higher power
This means the alcoholic has given their will and life over to God.

Step 4: Facing the problem
Now that the alcoholic has submitted to a higher power, it's time to face the music. Once they have done this, they can free themselves of the things that are stopping them from finding success.

Step 5: Confession to others
At this point, the alcoholic needs to admit to another person that they have a problem with alcohol. This may be one of the hardest steps because the addict has spent so much time in denial and will find it hard to admit they have an addiction to someone else. It's never easy to share your faults with others.

Step 6: Contemplation and preparation

At this point, the alcoholic will reflect on the previous steps and prepare themselves for the change they must make. God, as he knows Him, can now remove all their mentioned faults.

Step 7: Humbly ask God to free you from the addiction

Alcoholics will approach this step with great humility and ask God to free them from their flaws. In a way, they are asking to be exercised of their demons. They place their recovery in God's hands.

Step 8: Setting Things Right

This is similar to step 4, except instead of cleaning out their own closet of faults, they are trying to clean up the mess they have made with others. They will make a list of everyone they've harmed and the steps they can take to repair the relationship.

Step 9: Apologizing – Seeking forgiveness

Now that the alcoholic has made a list of those they've hurt and how they may patch things up, they have to follow through with their intentions. This may include paying back old debts, apologizing, or maybe even writing letters if the person would rather not speak with them. They must be sincere and make a true effort to mend the relationship they've damaged.

Step 10: Upkeep

This is a continuance of step 4. The alcoholic will proceed to make note of any new mistakes, feelings of fear, resentment or anger. Should any of these arise, they will once again ask God to purge them of these emotions.

Step 11: Prayer and meditation

Step 11 involves praying to God, as the alcoholic understands Him, and meditation. This helps maintain their spiritual relationship with this higher power.

Step 12: Helping Others

The twelfth step involves helping other alcoholics. Now that they are on the right path, they can help others reach their goal of sobriety. They have taken all the other 11 steps and have experience with the program. Most alcoholics find the greatest satisfaction from this pivotal step.

Detoxification for Both Alcoholics and Moderate Drinkers

Remember, alcohol is, in essence, a toxin and after awhile will build up in your system. You may be familiar with the idea of detoxing as it's popularized by the health industry. Typically, those who have consumed an abundance of processed, chemically ridden foods will cleanse their bodies of these toxins in order to feel refreshed and invigorated. The same can be done with alcohol, and you don't have to be an alcoholic to seek this treatment. If you're a moderate or social drinker, you may experience periods of fatigue, weakness, muscle aches, or even digestive issues. These are signs that you may be in need of a little detoxification.

If you haven't yet reached the point of dependency on alcohol, keep in mind that over time the substance may bring about kidney, liver and weight issues. It goes without saying that it could also cause addiction. Over time you will incur a serious accumulation of toxins in your body. While films and media have glorified the party lifestyle, excess use of alcohol will eventually take a grave toll on your health.

For those who are moderate or social drinkers, there are some things you can do to limit the long term effects of alcohol. If you are looking to detox, the easiest way to do so is to simply stop drinking. Eventually, your body will get rid of any remnants of the substance. Those who are heavier drinkers may find it easier to switch from hard liquor to something less potent, like wine, to begin. Generally, it's recommended that you abstain from alcohol use for up to one month, depending on how often you've been drinking. You may experience some withdrawal symptoms while detoxing. Some people have strong cravings for alcohol; others may experience nausea or anxiety.

By giving your body a much needed break from alcohol, you'll regain energy, increase your libido and maybe even lose a few pounds. After the detoxification process has finished, many people report feeling full of life and reinvigorated. It's suggested that you go the extra mile and also do a liver, kidney and colon cleanse. You may soon be amazed at how wonderful you feel after you've purged your body of all that poison.

Drinking While Pregnant – Never A Good Idea

As you can imagine, all of the harmful effects of alcohol would only be exacerbated by a pregnancy as it would also affect the fetus. Studies have shown that the use of alcohol during a pregnancy can cause heart or other organ defects, premature birth, a miscarriage or stillbirth. According to a study conducted in 2008, women who consumed five or more drinks per week had a 70% greater chance of having a stillborn than those who didn't drink (1). In some cases, drinking during pregnancy can cause neurological problems later on in the child's life.

When alcohol consumption affects a fetus, it is known as FAS (Fetal Alcohol Syndrome). Often times this is the cause of mental retardation in a child. In fact, it's the most common one. According to the CDC, approximately 1,000 to 6,000 babies in the United States are born with FAS each year (2). Children with this syndrome may be abnormally small at birth and have distinctive features, such as undersized eyes or a very thin upper lip. Emotional and/or behavioral problems often accompany these physical effects. In some cases, the heart fails to develop properly.

Some people may wonder if it's safe to drink at all during their pregnancy. Your doctor will likely advise you to abstain from drinking alcohol until after the baby is born. The truth is, no amount of alcohol has been proven to be harmless. The U.S. Surgeon General notes that consuming 7 or more alcoholic beverages per week puts the baby at the greatest risk (3). No matter the stage of pregnancy, there is a risk of mental retardation, or any of the above mentioned side effects. There's no concrete way to determine if consuming alcohol will or will not cause your baby any harm, so each time you have a drink you're playing Russian Roulette. FAS is permanent and can not be reversed.

The Link Between Alcohol and Cancer

It should come as no surprise that there is a link between alcohol and cancer, given its nature. While most people associate neglected alcoholism with cirrhosis of the liver, there is likewise a danger of developing cancer Studies have shown that males who consume two drinks a day and women who consume one have a greater risk of getting cancer. Because alcohol naturally causes harm to your body's cells, it acts as a breeding ground for cell division. Aside from this, it can also encourage enzymes to demolish vitamins and minerals that would otherwise act as cancer deterrents. Cancers of the throat, vocal cords and mouth are the most common. As a matter of fact, the American Cancer Society notes that oral cancers, such as those listed above are six times more likely to develop in alcohol users than non-alcohol users. Colon, liver, and breast cancer have also been known to stem from alcohol use. Avoiding any kind of alcoholic beverage will help reduce your chance of getting these kids of cancers.

It's hard to understand why people continue to consume large amounts of alcohol knowing that they can develop such a deadly disease. So, the next time you're invited to go out drinking, ask yourself whether or not it's worth the risk. This should be an easy answer if you subscribe to the theory that there is no cure for cancer. Nobody would want to chance having to endure months or years of such a painful illness.

Please try to remember that your body is well equipped to heal itself. This is what our immune system is built for. Of course, once we weaken the system, it becomes unable to function efficiently. Consumption of alcohol hinders the immune system, therefore, making it hard for the body to fight off illness.

So, what's the link to cancer here? Let's put this into perspective. While you inhibit your immune system, you are making it harder for your body to detect threats that it would normally destroy. Since alcohol use can encourage cell division and, in turn, cancerous cells, you are significantly impeding the chance that the immune system will pick up on it. If the body misses this cell and it's allowed to continue, it's develops into what we call cancer.

Engaging in behavior that hinders your immune system greatly increases your chance of falling ill. When you look at it in this way, it seems ludicrous to consume alcohol, or any other substance that is detrimental to your immune system. At the end of the day, it is up to you to decide if it's worth the risk. Whenever you drink, keep in mind that all of your body, including your immune system, gets drunk too.

Liver Cirrhosis: Another Health Risk of Alcoholism

Those who are dependent on alcohol suffer from an unforgiving and aggressive illness that affects both the mind and body. While so many horrible health risks have already been discussed, yet one more is the cirrhosis of the liver. It's the twelfth largest killer in the U.S., taking 26,000 lives annually. As you probably know, the liver is the largest organ inside the body. It's absolutely necessary that it functions efficiently in order to maintain health. The liver acts as a filter, removing unwanted toxins, bacteria and germs from the blood. However, it also creates special immune agents to combat illness, proteins that are responsible for blood clotting and bile that absorb fat soluble vitamins. When scar tissue replaces healthy tissue, cirrhosis occurs and causes blood flow to that organ to slow or stop altogether. This severely damages the liver's functioning.

Alcoholism is one of the leading causes of cirrhosis of the liver and is often thought of when discussing alcohol abuse. Those who have a long history of heavy drinking (10 years or more), stand the greatest risk of developing this condition. Of course each person is different, but it's been found that alcohol does cause harm to the liver by obstructing its metabolism. Some external symptoms include swelling of the abdomen and legs due to water accumulation. The technical terms for these conditions are edema (legs) and ascites (abdomen).

Cirrhosis can also cause you to bleed and bruise easier as your liver is unable to create the needed proteins to promote blood clotting. Often times, the sufferer will develop jaundice, yellowing of the skin and eyes, because the liver cannot retain ample amounts of bilirubin. Because your liver is unable to filter out the body's toxins, it's possible to develop sepsis which can lead to organ failure and death. These poisons can cause mental malfunctions or even coma.

As you can see, alcohol dependence is not something to be taken lightly. When neglected, it will eventually lead to serious health complications. However, it is a condition that is both preventable and treatable with determination, professional help and the right recovery program. So long as the environment and all those inside of it are devoted to getting the alcoholic back on track, most of these health risks can be avoided. Given that cirrhosis of the liver is directly, although not exclusively, linked to alcoholism, treating alcohol dependence as early as possible is key.

Alcohol Detox: Cleansing Your Body

Chances are you've had a little too much to drink at least once in your life. This may be during the holidays, some other special occasion, or even just a gathering with friends to celebrate the weekend. Depending on the person, this may happen once or twice a year, but in other cases it may happen once or twice per week. While this may be troubling to others, they haven't reached the point where they are dependent on alcohol and still maintain control over their use of the substance.

Just because they haven't become addicted to alcohol, doesn't mean they aren't damaging their bodies. The more you consume, the more harm you bring upon yourself. Each time you consume an alcoholic beverage, your body immediately starts working to combat and destroy the toxins from the substance. Whether you're a moderate drinker, or occasional, it's good to regularly do a thorough cleansing of those built up poisons.

Did you know that after just one drink, your liver can actually become swollen? An excess amount of water and fat globules can bring this on. This condition is often referred to as "fatty liver." Aside from alcohol use, this condition can be caused by other medical conditions like obesity or diabetes. Certain drugs can also bring on a fatty liver. When this condition is caused by alcohol, it can be reversed by abstaining from alcohol use. You can help your liver reverse this condition and function properly through a cleanse of your body.

So, if the liver is negatively affected by alcohol use, chances are the kidneys will be as well. Kidneys act as another filter for your body, eliminating waste and regulating both fluids and electrolytes. By nature, alcohol is a diuretic and therefore can cause dehydration. If your body is dehydrated, your kidneys find it hard to function efficiently and manage electrolytes. The kidneys are not taking any direct damage, per say, but will struggle to work properly while your intoxicated. Those who are heavy drinkers risk kidney failure. A good cleanse will also help your kidneys get back into shape and eliminate any waste that's accrued.

Moderate quantities of alcohol can also stop your digestive system from breaking down and taking in nutrients. Your intestines are vital, as they are what eliminate waste from the body and absorb essential vitamins and minerals. It's crucial this organ functions properly in order to maintain a healthy and balanced body. Just as a cleanse will aid your liver and kidneys, it will do the same for your intestines.

These "filters" within your body need to be maintained and cleansed much like filters that come with your household appliances. Have you ever pulled out your dryer's lint filter, only to find there's so much lint you can't even find the filter itself? How can your appliance function properly when there's so much "gunk" in the way? In the case of the dryer filter, excess build-up can cause a fire! And while your body will certainly not catch fire, you will begin to feel sluggish or even develop illnesses if your body becomes clogged up with toxins.

This is why cleansing should be part of your regular routine. You want to ensure that your body is in tip top shape and optimally functioning. Whether you only have a drink once or twice a month, or you make it a weekly event, regular cleansing will help keep your body free of the substance's toxins. It might be a good idea to start with a colon cleanse and then work your way to a liver and kidney cleanse.

If you're up for it, you can also do a full body cleanse. These are typically two week programs and can be purchased at most health and grocery stores, as well as pharmacies. Some of the full body cleanses involve taking pills, while others involve drinking a specially formulated tea. These will purge your body of those toxins that you've built up throughout your lifetime. Yes, you may have some toxins that have been there since adolescence. Because these cleansers are so powerful, you should consult your physician before starting such a program as it can affect your medication. While you are cleansing, be sure to drink lots of water, ideally ½ your body weight in ounces, daily. You'll also want to include more fiber to really help get all of the toxins out. Lentils, beans, artichokes and raspberries are all fiber rich foods.

While there are so many harmful side effects of alcohol, there are so many more positive side effects of a full body cleanse. One of these positives is weight loss. Because you're removing toxins, build-up in the colon and intestines and flushing out excess water, you will probably shed a few pounds. While it's not dramatic, it can definitely be a boost to your motivation.

Many people report a boost in energy and positive change in their mood after going through a cleanse. This is surely your body thanking you for getting rid of all that heavy toxic waste in your system!

Alcohol: A Glass a Day for Heart Health?

There's been a lot of buzz lately about how the consumption of alcohol, specifically red wine, can actually be good for your heart. A glass a day, so they say. This kind of headline will certainly get the attention of the public as most of us want a good reason to carry out seemingly bad behavior. It's okay to pour that glass of wine, it's good for you!

However, when you really dissect the information released, you find quite a few holes that leave you wondering whether or not you'll just wind up hurting your body, rather than helping it. Furthermore, some people take this kind of a story too far and go overboard with their alcohol consumption. Alcoholics may see this as just one more reason to keep on drinking. In fact, most of those studies never even mention the harmful effects of alcohol abuse and lead the reader to believe that these benefits apply to both women and men. Unfortunately, this is just not the case.

A lot of the research involving alcohol's ability to raise HDL levels, or good cholesterol, only factors in males and post-menopausal females. How about young females? Truthfully, there has been little proof that alcohol consumption is beneficial for younger women. Studies suggest that, in fact, younger women who consume alcohol are more likely to develop disease.

The British Journal of Cancer reported in 2002 that alcohol use was the root cause of up to 4% of breast cancer cases (4). This same report, which analyzed 63 related studies, found that 65% of those studies established a link between breast cancer and the use of alcohol. Each drink that a woman consumes only increases her risk of breast cancer.

Given our society's fixation on appearance, perhaps the fact that alcohol use can cause weight gain might gain your attention. The Centers for Disease Control and Prevention (CDC) estimates that over 60% of women are overweight or obese (5). If you fall into this group, adding alcohol to your diet will only be detrimental to your weight loss efforts. Even if you're part of the 40% who are not overweight, you may soon find yourself there should you add or continue to consume alcohol to your diet.

There's approximately 25 calories in each ounce of red wine. Doesn't sound like much, right? The typical restaurant glass of wine is 5 ounces, which equals 125 calories per glass. Three glasses later and you've taken in 375 calories! Of course if you're having a glass at home, you may be pouring even more than 5 ounces in each glass.

This adds up pretty quickly if you're drinking regularly. It also makes calorie counting a nightmare as now you're a little too tipsy to be judging how much alcohol you've poured into your glass. What's even worse is that because alcohol lowers your inhibition, you are likely to overeat. Alcohol also curbs your metabolism for up to one day.

At the end of the day, you need to use some common sense and be truthful with yourself. Is it really okay to go out and binge drink this weekend just because a study says some alcohol consumption can be heart healthy? Alcohol is not like vegetables in that it if a little is good, more must be better. You now have an understanding of the harmful effects of excessive alcohol use, so why put your body at risk? Eat a healthy diet, exercise regularly and maintain a positive attitude. These are the things that will keep your heart healthy. The antioxidants found in fruits and vegetables will keep your "ticker" strong and reduce your cholesterol naturally.

It's important to do your research, especially when you're talking about what is and what isn't healthy. So, the next time your friends ask you to go out for a few drinks, remember the phrase, "everything in moderation."

References

1.	Aliyu, M.H., et al. Alcohol Consumption During Pregnancy and the Risk of Early Stillbirth among Singletons. Alcohol, volume 42, August 2008, pages 369-374.

2.	Bertrand, J., et al., National Task Force on FAS/FAE. Fetal Alcohol Syndrome: Guidelines for Referral and Diagnosis. Atlanta, GA: Centers for Disease Control and Prevention, July 2004.

3.	Surgeon General. Surgeon General's Advisory on Alcohol Use in Pregnancy. February 21, 2005.

4.	"Alcohol, Tobacco and Breast Cancer – Collaborative Reanalysis of Individual Data from 53 Epidemiological Studies, including 58 515 Women with Breast Cancer and 95 067 Women without the Disease." British Journal of Cancer 87.11 (2002): 1234-245. British Journal of Cancer. Web. 22 Mar. 2012.

5.	Ogden, Ph.D., Cynthia L., and Margaret D. Carroll, M.S.P.H. "Prevalence of Overweight, Obesity, and Extreme Obesity Among Adults: United States, Trends 1960–1962 Through 2007–2008." Centers for Disease Control and Prevention(2010). Centers for Disease Control and Prevention. Web. 22 Mar. 2012.